THE HOLMANS OF CANTERBURY

The family firm that
traded in Dover Street for
one hundred and fifty years

Written and researched by Shena Fielding, Peta McFarlane,
Michael Steed, Sheila Tyler and Mary Wood members of the
Local History Group of the Oaten Hill and District Society

HOLMAN WINDMILLS IN EAST KENT

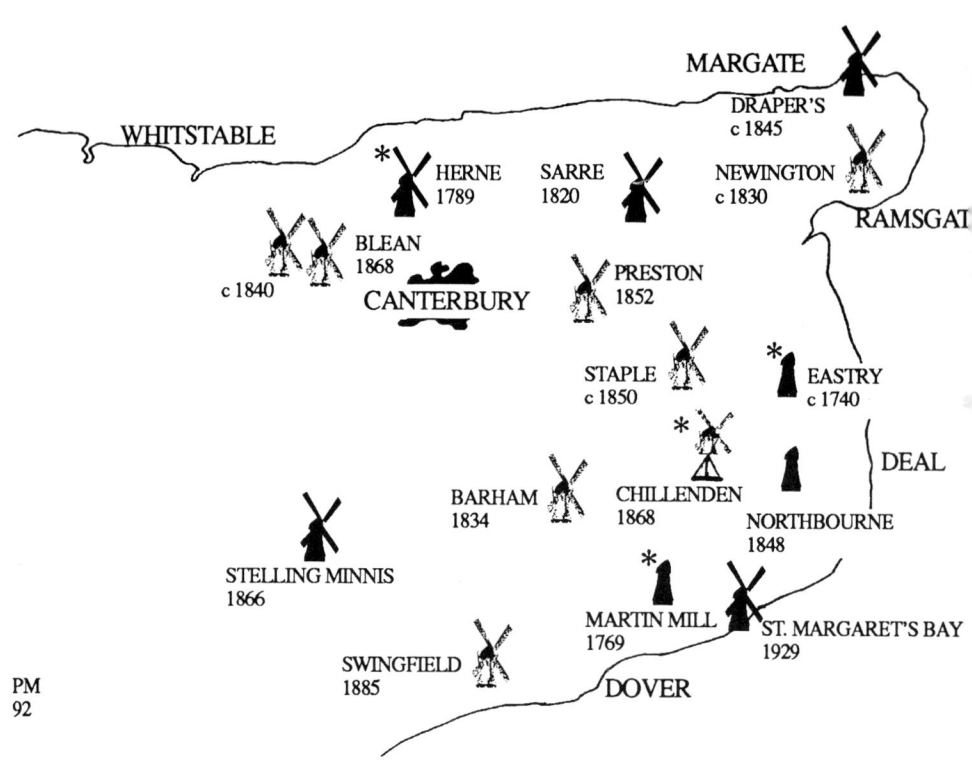

	five Holman-built mills still standing, one without sweeps
	seven Holman-built mills no longer standing
	a mill still standing maintained by Holmans but not built by them
	a post mill still standing maintained by Holmans but not built by them
	two mills still standing now without sweeps maintained by Holmans but not built by them

DETAILS OF VISITING ARRANGEMENTS MAY BE OBTAINED FROM:-

DRAPER'S MILL	0843 226227
HERNE MILL	0227 361326
SARRE MILL	0843 47573
STELLING MINNIS	0227 87635

THE HOLMANS OF CANTERBURY

Tom Holman and his sister Mary talked to us of their father, Harry Branford Holman; he told them of their grandfather Thomas Richard, of the family business in Dover Street (earlier known as Dover Lane) and of some of the men who had worked there up to the closure of the firm in 1975. We have spoken with many of these employees and have heard of the tools and machinery they used, the variety of services and the conditions of work. They told us, too, of some of the places they visited in maintaining windmills, watermills, wells and farm machinery. We have tried to gather up the threads from all these sources and weave them into this story of the Holmans.

Let us go back to the beginning. The firm dates from 1816, when Tom's great-grandfather, John, set up in business as a millwright and wheelwright. No records survive from its early decades and all we knew to start with was that, aged 32, he took over an existing firm from Widow Hunns and that he had previously worked for nearly ten years for Sweetloves of Wingham. But we didn't know what he did before then, where he lived, why he had apparently served no apprenticeship in his craft, how he acquired his skills and his capital, plus the ability and confidence to manage a business. Successful family businesses, such as Holmans of Canterbury were for a century and a half, do not fall out of the sky.

The Holman family has one intriguing clue: a document written in 1800 by Captain Holman of Ramsgate for Mr. Holman, miller of Ramsgate, though nothing in the document itself proves a connection with John Holman of Dover Street or explains why it ended up in the possession of his descendants. With evidence from church registers and other records held in the Cathedral archives and in the C.P. Davies collection of material on mills held in the Templeman Library at the University of Kent we believe that we have found the link: the Ramsgate miller was the elder brother of the founder of Holmans of Canterbury. We have used these various sources to explore further John Holman's background.

Captain Holman traced the family origins to an Arthur Holman who came from Dorset to the Isle of Thanet in 1564, settling in St. Nicholas-at-Wade where his descendants established themselves as gentry and were recognised by a coat of arms. The main branch moved to Ramsgate and became seafarers; Captain Holman (who died in May 1816, aged 82) became a ship's master and a man of substance in the town.

According to Captain Holman, our John Holman was descended from a younger brother of the Captain's grandfather. At some point this branch of the family went into milling. We found a tantalising reference to a miller Holman at St. Nicholas in 1624, and a trail of subsequent clues to Holmans, sometimes millers, in Sarre, Chislet and Westbere, which may have been the route which led John's father William to become the miller at Boughton under Blean.

John's childhood cannot have been easy. His mother died just before Christmas 1787 when he was four and there is no record of his father remarrying. To this was added the difficulties of a father's failing business. The advertisement shown opposite is the first of a series in the Kentish Gazette leading to the liquidation of William Holman's milling business in November 1794. We do not know where the ten year old boy, his siblings and father went next; clues point to Chartham and to Ramsgate where his brother William was a miller by 1800. We have a probable identification of another brother Charles, a ship's carpenter living in Ramsgate in 1813. So John may well have spent some years in Ramsgate, perhaps working in his brother's mill or even going to sea for a period before going to Sweetloves in 1806.

Thus we can form a picture of a boy who, watching his father work the Boughton mill, found a fascination for windmills which became his love and his life; whose father could not afford to pay for his apprenticeship when he was in his teens; but who developed his skills through a supportive family and may, along with his brothers, have been helped by the better off Ramsgate Holmans. The trades chosen by three brothers, miller, carpenter and millwright, do suggest a family pattern. All three appear to have learned from their father's misfortunes and prospered. By the time John Holman died he owned Draper's Mill and a house at Margate, as well as his Dover Street business.

We still do not know how John Holman managed to buy Mrs. Hunns' firm; even though unmarried, it cannot have been easy to save from a worker's wage at Sweetloves. The courteous notice in the Kentish Chronicle appears to us to have been put in by both of them. But there are several signs that it took a few years for John Holman to get his own business going.

Kentish Gazette

To be SOLD by AUCTION,
At the FLEUR DE LIS, HIGH-STREET, CANTERBURY,
On MONDAY the 12d day of July, 1791,
between the hours of three and five o'clock in the Afternoon, unless disposed of sooner by Private contract, of which notice will be given,

A Valuable FREEHOLD WINDMILL, situate near the street, in the parish of BOUGHTON BLEAN, now in the occupation of Mr. WM. HOLMAN. The Purchaser may have immediate possession.

For further particulars apply to Mr. NEWPORT, Wheelwright, Dover Lane, Canterbury.

Kentish Chronicle

MRS. HUNNS,
BROAD-STREET, CANTERBURY,

BEGS leave to return her thanks to her Friends for the favours conferred on her late husband, and solicits to recommend Mr. JOHN HOLMAN to their notice, who has lately taken the Business of her.

JOHN HOLMAN, MILLWRIGHT,

Begs leave to solicit the favours of the late Mr. HUNNS's employers and others, who may please to favour him with their commands, and informs them that he intends carrying on the above business in all its branches: having been in the employ of Messrs. Sweetloves', of Wingham, nearly ten years, he trusts, by paying a strict attention to execute the orders he may receive, to merit a continuance of their favors and support, which will be most gratefully acknowledged by their most obedient servant.

N. B.—Two Winnowing Machines for Sale on an improved principle

Northgate, Canterbury. Jan. 29, 1816.

The tithe records of St. Mary's Northgate show John Holman paying a small rate from 1816 to 1821, presumably on the Hunns' modest shop in Broad Street. But on 2nd February 1822 John Holman purchased his freemanship of the City of Canterbury, an indication of a growing prosperity. A year later he married, just a month short of his fortieth birthday. Was this late marriage because he decided to wait until he could support a family, the sign of a prudence learned the hard way in childhood, which also profited him in business?

By 1824 he is listed in Pigot's directory as a millwright in Dover Lane, along with Newports the wheelwrights, who were mentioned in the 1793 auction notice. Whether this early link brought him to Dover Street we do not know, but whatever did so served the firm well. Holmans, as they later developed into agricultural engineers, found themselves conveniently near the cattle market and farmers' meeting places in Canterbury such as the Flying Horse Inn.

We believe that Sarre Mill really launched John Holman's career. We found existing published sources crediting him with both this mill in 1820 and Herne Mill in 1789 (when he was aged six!). Was there another John Holman? In any case accurate dating of a mill can be unreliable as in the olden days it was not uncommon for a mill to be transferred either bodily or in sections from one site where it was no longer of use, to another, perhaps to replace a mill which had been damaged or totally destroyed by some disaster or by sheer neglect. Mills have always been exceptionally vulnerable; their exposed positions result in constant buffeting from storms and high winds and as the majority of their construction is of timber, fire is a constant hazard.

Though Sarre Mill bears the date 1820, documentary evidence points to an earlier Sarre Mill built by another John Holman, the local miller (who died in 1826) who must also have been something of a millwright. We have discovered (from his son's will) that he was our John Holman's uncle. Could he have been the builder of Herne Mill in 1789 as well? His own will shows a close connection with that mill; if so, his six-year old nephew may even have been there when it was built.

The 1820 building of Sarre Mill was partly a reconstruction: Malcolm Hobbs, who has recently restored it, tells us that a substantial proportion of the timber had been re-used and some beams had previously been windmill sweeps. Certainly the building of Sarre Mill has all the hallmarks of a family enterprise. We can still see inscribed on the bricks of the base of the mill, along with the date 1820, the initials T.H. (probably Thomas Holman, son of John the miller; Thomas later became the miller of Sarre until his death in 1867) and H.J.H. (was this Harry Jones Holman of Littlebourne, first cousin both to our John and to Thomas?).

Sarre was said to be "eight miles from anywhere" being eight miles from Canterbury, from Margate, from Ramsgate and from Sandwich. In 1854 it was heightened by Thomas Richard Holman to gain more advantage from the wind. The whole wooden structure was raised on jacks and the brick base was then built up under it by some eight to nine feet. In 1861 it was the first windmill in Kent to have a steam engine installed to help to turn the sweeps on windless days. This was replaced by a gas engine in 1907; the last of the Holman family (Holman Steddy) ceased to run the mill when he was commissioned in 1914; in 1920 the mill stopped working by power; by 1940 it had stopped completely and was left to decay; but the building found a different use during World War II as an observation tower.

But, in 1985, Malcolm Hobbs and his son, Robert, took it over and have painstakingly brought the mill back to life. So, today, visitors can go to the smock mill in Sarre; they can explore every part of the interior and read on the plaque HOLMAN BROS CANTERBURY. When the wind is right and the sweeps are turning fast they marvel at man's ingenuity at harnessing the power of the wind.

Chillenden Post Mill

However the earliest of English windmills were post mills in which the whole body of the mill turned on its post to face the wind. One example is Chillenden Mill built in 1868 and maintained by Holman Bros during the nineteen twenties. But smock mills rely on a cap rotated by means of a fantail to catch the wind to change the position of the sweeps ('sweeps' being the Kentish word for the sails of a windmill). Smock mills are so called as they look like traditionally dressed country folk striding along the hilltops.

"A hundred years ago windmills and watermills were sights so common they were hardly noticed. Today few are left, and their numbers are still diminishing." This quotation from the Society for the Protection of Ancient Buildings is all too true. The Holman windmills are a proud part of our national heritage. Sarre was the first of many smock mills built by John Holman, his sons and grandsons. Four still stand, three of which can be explored by the public.

Draper's Smock Mill at Margate was built by John Holman in 1845 and worked by wind power until 1916. In 1927 the sweeps and fantail were removed, a twenty horse power gas engine was installed and the mill continued to grind grain until the mid-thirties when it fell into decay. The Kent County Council acquired the whole property in 1968 and Mr R. M. Towers, the Headmaster of the adjacent school, saddened by the proposal to demolish the mill, set up the Draper's Windmill Trust which has been responsible for its eventual restoration. The staging, originally intended for Barham Mill which burnt down in November 1969, was donated to the Trust by the K.C.C. In the spring of 1975 the work was completed and the four sweeps once more turned to grind corn.

Draper's Mill, Margate

Stelling Minnis Mill

Stelling Minnis is a fine black tarred smock mill standing on the site of an earlier post mill which was pulled down in 1866 to make way for this new mill built by Thomas Richard Holman. It was restored in 1935 the work being carried out by his sons and grandsons. In 1878 the mill had been bought by Henry Davison and it stayed in the same family for a hundred years. Its last owner, Alec Davison, was using wind power for grinding grain for animal feed to within a few months of his death in 1970. But shortly before this he had bequeathed the mill to the K.C.C. and it is now maintained by the Stelling Minnis Parish Council and the East Kent Mills Group.

The last smock mill to have been built in Kent and the last one built by Holman Bros was in 1929 on the cliff top at St Margaret's Bay. It was commissioned by Sir William Beardswell to be the centre-piece of an unusual design of house and was never intended for corn grinding. However to provide work for the mill to do a belt driven DC dynamo was installed to generate domestic electricity. It is very slightly smaller than a normal windmill but its design by Harry Branford Holman is correct in every detail. Although this mill cannot be visited by the public nevertheless it is a striking landmark on the South Foreland cliffs near the lighthouse.

St Margaret's Bay Mill

Barham Mill

A well-remembered mill of John Holman's was the one at Barham built in 1834 to succeed an old post mill of the sixteenth century. A mill at Barham was actually recorded in the Doomsday Book of 1086. John Holman's was known as the Black Mill being covered by tarred sheeting which preserved it so well that there was no change in its appearance right up to the time when it was sadly burnt down - sad for the local people who can no longer say "there's always been a windmill on Barham Downs". It was said that the miller at Preston Mill, near Wingham, after a period of calm weather, could judge when his mill would be favoured with a breeze to set her sweeps in motion when he could see those of Barham revolving, "Barham is off!"

However the earliest smock mill still standing that has been worked on by the Holmans is the one at Herne built in 1789. It was always described as a "very hard worker". In 1856 the whole structure was raised seventeen feet to take greater advantage of the prevailing wind and the mill continued to run until 1952 when it stopped working by wind power and electrical milling equipment was installed. Today this mill can be visited and is another one owned by the K.C.C. It is now managed by the Friends of Herne Mill.

Herne Mill

HOLMAN FREEMEN OF THE CITY OF CANTERBURY	
JOHN HOLMAN	1822
JOHN JAMES HOLMAN	1854
THOMAS RICHARD HOLMAN	1854
HARRY BRANFORD HOLMAN	1885
WILLIAM JOHN HOLMAN	1886
JOHN ANGELL HOLMAN	1936
FRANK HOLMAN	1955

The two sons of John Holman

Thomas Richard   *John James*

But before we leave the grand old days of windmills, if you should go to Jerusalem you can find there on the outskirts of the city a windmill bearing a plaque saying HOLMANS OF CANTERBURY. This unique mill which has figured on Israeli postage stamps and bank notes was commissioned by Sir Moses Montefiore the Jewish benefactor who at one time lived at Ramsgate. It still stands as yet another example of the skills and reputation of Holman's millwrights. A description of its building is opposite.

Illustrated London News 1858

The windmill at Jerusalem 1857

Extracts from T R Holman's Obituary Notice
Death of Well-known Engineer

"We regret to announce the death on Sunday 28th November 1897 age 66 of Thomas Richard Holman, chief of the well-known firm of Canterbury engineers. He was held in the highest respect and esteem.

For a time he followed the profession of millwright. The introduction of steam power, however, caused a revolution in milling work and engineering was afterwards added.

Early in the year 1857 Mr Thomas Holman and his brother were employed by Sir Moses Montefiore to erect a windmill at Jerusalem under the direction of the Society for Assisting the Jews. Mr T R Holman went out to superintend the work, taking a foreman with him, and employing Arab labour. The machinery was all made and fitted at the works in Dover Street, sent by sea to Jaffa, and there landed with much difficulty in small boats. There were no roads and no carriages - all was taken on camels, with a guide leading the way, and Mr Holman following on horseback.

It was the custom of the Arabs to demand "Backsheesh" every morning before beginning labour, and Jews came down in great numbers to curse the work which was going on. It took about 18 months to complete the mill. At the end of that time, Mr Holman went down to Jaffa to inspect the wells in connection with the irrigation of the orange gardens there. This inspection brought on Syrian fever of the most dangerous type, but he was successfully attended and nursed by an American lady doctor.

Mr Holman returned to England in 1858.

Some years after this he was employed by a German firm to send out machinery for the erection of a windmill at Haifa, on Mount Carmel in Syria, a then thriving German colony. On this occasion one important piece of machinery was lost in the sea owing to the difficulty of landing heavy goods at Jaffa.

Nearly every mill in the County of Kent has at some time or other been either refitted with machinery or repaired from the Dover Street works.

There were many present at the Funeral to pay a last tribute to a respected citizen."

Swingfield Mill 1885 - the last cornmill to be constructed in Kent. It was built by William John Holman who is seen standing on the staging with his father Thomas Richard Holman.

Tom Holman writes of this time: "Towards the latter part of the nineteenth century there was a change in the work done by the firm as although much was still done in mills the coming of steam power and later the internal combustion engine meant additional work. Many mills had the new form of power to keep the mill turning during periods of little wind. Another change was the increasing involvement in the agricultural side of the business and whilst the firm had previously made the old wooden Kent turnwrest plough in their workshops the tendency was now for the sale of iron implements such as ploughs, mowers, reapers and horse rakes made in factories in England and America."

Ploughing with Overtime tractor in the early twenties

So the middle of the nineteenth century saw the start of a period of exciting and rapid change both for John Holman's business and for the farmers it served. His younger son, Thomas Richard, was educated at the Dane John Academy in Canterbury which he left when he was fifteen years old to become apprenticed to his father.

> EXTRACT FROM APPRENTICESHIP INDENTURE 11TH NOVEMBER 1846
> THOMAS R. HOLMAN TO JOHN HOLMAN
>
> "This Indenture witnesseth that THOMAS RICHARD HOLMAN, son of JOHN HOLMAN of the City of Canterbury Millwright of his own accord doth put himself Apprentice to the said John Holman to learn his Art and with him after the manner of an Apprentice to serve from the First day of May now past unto the full End And Terms of Seven years...during which Term the said apprentice his said Master faithfully shall and will serve his Secrets keep and his lawful Commands everywhere gladly to....
>
> The Goods of his Master he shall not waste, nor lend them unlawfully to any; Hurt to his Master he shall not do, cause or procure to be done; he shall neither buy nor sell without his Masters Licence; Taverns, Inns or Alehouses he shall not haunt; at Cards, Dice, Tables or any other unlawful Game he shall not play, nor from the Service of his said Master Day or Night absent himself, but in all things as an honest and faithful Apprentice shall and will demean and behave himself towards his Master and all his Family during all the said Term And the said John Holman in consideration of the natural love and affection which he hath and beareth towards his said Son and of the work and labour to be done and performed by him doth promise and agree that he the said John Holman the said Apprentice in the Art, Trade Mystery or Business of a Millwright which he now useth shall teach and instruct or cause to be taught and instructed, after the best Way and Manner that he can finding and allowing unto the said Apprentice sufficient Meat, Drink, Lodging, Wearing Apparel and all other necessaries fit for an apprentice during the Term aforesaid.
>
> In Witness hereof, the Parties abovesaid to these Indenture interchangeably have set their Hands and Seals, the Eleventh Day of November in the tenth Year of the Reign of our Sovereign Lady Victoria by the Grace of God, of the United Kingdom of Great Britain and Ireland, Queen, Defender of the Faith etc., and in the Year of our Lord One Thousand Eight Hundred and Forty Six."
>
> THOMAS RICHARD HOLMAN
> JOHN HOLMAN

The two sons, John James and Thomas Richard came of age in the early 1850s and in 1854 the firm took the name of Holman & Sons. Their father died the next year, so the two brothers had full responsibility for the firm's fortunes thrust upon them just as it was expanding and changing in character. A large new workshop was constructed in Dover Street and the firm became "Engineers, Millwrights & Wheelwrights" in 1855. Fortunately for them the 1850s were times of great agricultural prosperity; harvests were good, the new railways encouraged farmers in East Kent to grow more, sending their produce to London and increasing profits enabled go-ahead farmers to pay for new technology.

As the two brothers took over, the rapid surge in the use of steam power on farms was getting under way - first steam threshing machines, which were still dependent on four legged horse-power to be taken to farms and then mobile steam engines which could move from farm to farm by their own power. Traction engines were used in pairs for ploughing. The sight and sound of such massive machines on the inadequate country roads was so awe inspiring that in 1861 Parliament passed a law limiting the speed of mechanically propelled vehicles on the public highway to two m.p.h. and requiring a man with a red flag to walk six hundred yards in front to warn people and horses. There was an occasion when Holmans had a traction engine working in a field too near to a public road and because they had omitted to take the precaution of notifying the police beforehand they received a summons.

We cannot know what the two brothers thought of these dramatic changes or whether they realised that just as steam power was offering them new business with farmers, the substitution of steam power for wind power in milling was about to send the firm's original business into a long decline. Many would have stuck to their familiar trade, and with the commission to go out and build that windmill in Jerusalem, the two young men could have been forgiven for thinking there would be plenty more work of that sort. Instead Holmans diversified their business just at the right time and seem to have been in the vanguard of those firms who were investing in sets of machines to hire out to farmers. But, during the three decades after 1870, there was severe agricultural depression, especially in cereal production, and many steam plough contractors went under. Holmans kept going and in a large area of North East Kent farmers looked to Dover Street not only for their ploughing and threshing but for their agricultural equipment, repairs and maintenance of farm machinery.

After the Franco Prussian War of 1870-71 steam traction engines and ploughing tackle were sent from the South East of England to France to help plough up the battlefields near Metz - this project was organised by the Societé Britannique de Sécours aux Paysans. It would be fascinating to know whether Holmans were involved in this most unusual assignment but unfortunately we have found no records in England or in France to give us more details.

Members of the Holman Family who feature in this Booklet

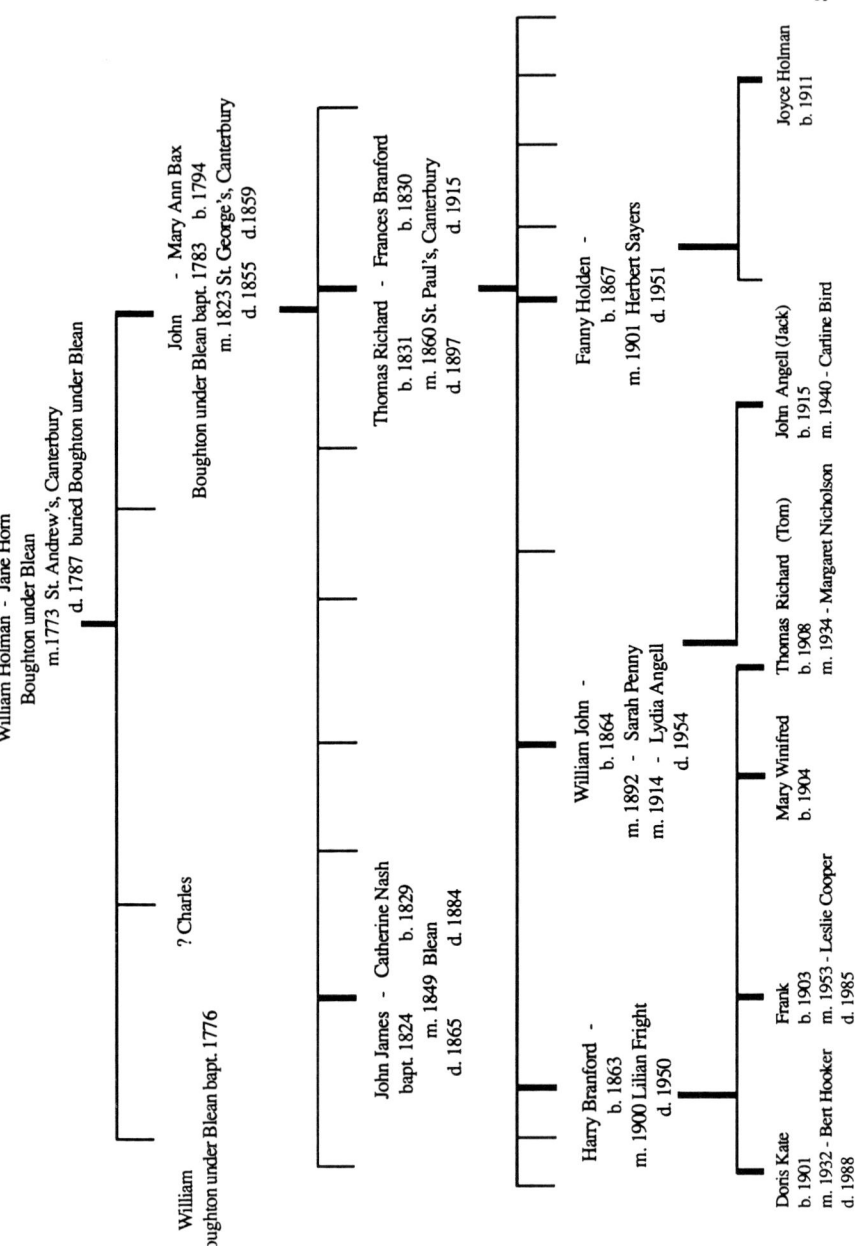

Harry Branford Holman and his wife Lilian with their children Doris, Frank, Mary and Tom about 1914

By the end of the nineteenth century Holman Bros. were, in the words of a later employee, 'able to tackle anything'. Harry Branford and William John, the generation on from John James and Thomas Richard, were taking their places in the firm. John Holman had set this pattern of a family firm when he took his two sons into the business and the pattern continued throughout the years. In the home the family was the mainspring and support of its members who were working in Dover Street. Tom and Mary in their early memories give us a graphic picture of their home, of their school days and of everyday life in Canterbury.

Their father, Harry Branford, married Lilian Fright in 1900 and their first home was at 12 Vernon Place. In 1908 they moved to 38 Nunnery Fields, a house called Belle Vue Villas, where they lived for the next fifty years and where the children, Doris, Frank, Mary and Tom, grew up. Tom describes the four-storeyed house as Victorian with a semi-basement kitchen which was fitted with a gas stove although the old Kitchener range was still there and was used to cook the 25lb turkey at Christmas time, the more modern gas stove being far too small. The house was lit by gas but everyone went to bed by candlelight. The furniture was mostly of a heavy Victorian type and the decoration rather plain and dull. He remembers, quite vividly, the marble-topped wash-stand in the front bedroom which was used as an operating table when the local doctor removed his adenoids.

The family home - No 38 Nunnery Fields

Mary told us that they didn't buy a refrigerator until 1950; before that to keep the milk fresh in summer they would put the jug of milk under a large earthenware jar or even under a flower pot covered with a wet cloth to cool by evaporation. They had a live-in maid and a Mrs. Bean came on a Monday morning to do the washing when a fire was lit under the copper.

Mary went on to describe her mother's clothes as always being "full length and waisted; discreet blouses with net filling-in at the neck. Her hats really were hats - worthy of the name! My sister and I wore starched sun bonnets of broderie anglaise in the summer and the boys wore sailor hats. We always wore pinafores of course. I shall never forget wearing those woolly combinations which we had to change on a Sunday morning - I'd have worn the same combinations for ever rather than change into clean ones as they tickled so! We also had grey cotton stays and a flannel petticoat and then a white petticoat on top. It was my father who was responsible for buying our shoes and this was always a great outing. We were taken down to Orchard's in the High Street at the end of St. Margaret's Street. How I longed for a pair of boy's boots which had a little tag at the back to pull them on but I was never allowed to have these although I always remember wearing boots as a child."

In those days most tradesmen called at the house for the weekly orders. The milkman came three times a day; he made his rounds in a milk float 'rather like a chariot' drawn by a horse; the milk was in large cans into which he dipped a ladle and filled his customers' jugs. Every Saturday morning on the way to his office, Harry Branford called at Hills' the butcher at the bottom of Nunnery Fields to order the joint; this was delivered by half past ten ready to be cooked in time for lunch.

There was a great distinction at that time between living in Nunnery Fields and South Canterbury Road - Mary said "South Canterbury was a cut above Nunnery Fields and we were almost the last house before the turning leading to Nunnery Fields Hospital. This road was known as Union Road and it led to what was then the Workhouse and from our windows we could see the Union garden and the Labour Master supervising the work. We would watch the tramps sitting on the bank by the hedge of The Pines opposite our house as they counted or hid their money before going into the Workhouse for the night. If any of these 'casuals' wanted breakfast they had to do an hour's stint in the Union garden. As they left tramps often asked at No. 38 for boiling water to fill their teacans and I expect they were usually given the tea to go with it as well." Tom recalled that stretching from the Workhouse grounds to the Elham Valley railway line were Fowler's orchards, "the domain of the cuckoo in early summer and of human bird scarers when the cherries were ripe." The view from the Holmans' house was in Mary's words, "very countrified and lovely; nothing but orchards as we looked out towards Wincheap and beyond that the river Stour which was always flooding the meadows and then right on to Harbledown where in my youth there was a windmill - it was a real landmark."

This Elham Valley railway generated a great deal of excitement. From the top windows of No. 38 the train could be seen leaving Canterbury West Station and coming along the high embankment up to the little Canterbury South Station. If someone left the house when it was first seen there was just time to run to the station to catch it. This was a well-remembered event by Mary who travelled to Folkestone on this line for the final years of her schooldays.

Doris, Frank, Mary and Tom all went to the Simon Langton Schools which were at that time between St. George's Street, Gravel Lane and Rose Lane. A plaque on the wall of the Whitefriars opening in St. George's Street marks the old entrance to both the Boys' and Girls' Schools which were badly damaged during the Second World War. Mary who was there between 1909 and 1918 remembers that "discipline was fairly strict - I know I was always in trouble and used to get detention, unlike my sister who was a model pupil. Miss Proudfoot was the Headmistress and looking back I think the school was very up-to-date and quite go ahead. Of course we had no contact with the boys - we were not even allowed to look at each other. When the boys had a new gym built the girls were allowed to use this on certain days in the week and we were taken over in 'croc' but not allowed to look to the right or to the left. We didn't wear a uniform but at the end of the summer term there was always a commemoration service in the Cathedral when we had to wear white dresses, with long sleeves of course, and we had to wear a sprig of ivy. Why we wore ivy I have no idea but we always did."

Tom Holman and his father at Sarre Mill 1920

Recalling his schooldays at the Simon Langton Boys' School, Tom told us "There was school on Saturday mornings but Saturday and Wednesday afternoons were holidays and once a month there was a Saturday morning off which was called a Merit Holiday for good behaviour but which could be forfeited." The Headmaster then was J. J. Sharp and fees were 4 guineas a term, and classrooms had names such as Faraday (the chemistry laboratory) Newton (the physics laboratory) and Ruskin (the art room). There was a Cadet Corps organised and members paraded in the playground after school and used the indoor and outdoor ranges. Tom continued, "Our playing fields were on a triangular piece of ground bounded by Nackington Road, the Elham Valley railway and the diagonal footpath; later there was a field off Sturry Road somewhere near Barton Mill. We swam at the open-air swimming pool in Whitehall which was always advertised as the largest open-air bath in Kent being 125 yards long and 25 yards wide, but I cannot think that the quality of the water would come up to present day standards -the water came from the river and my father's firm had the job once a year of sending a steam engine and pump down to empty the bath out so that it could be scrubbed and cleaned." The girls went to the indoor swimming baths in Station Road West. Mary said "Our early swimming costumes were 'skinny' ones which came right down to our knees, with sleeves almost down to your elbow."

For holidays the Holman family would often take a house at Tankerton. The popular way to travel there was to cycle and all the children had bicycles. Tom remembers his father's car - at that time a model 'T' Ford which was used strictly for business purposes. "He would take the family out in it on Bank Holidays but he would never drive on a Sunday."

Mary has some First World War memories - "I was ten years old but I can remember very well that Canterbury was a garrison town and of course was full of soldiers. At 9 o'clock on Sunday mornings there was a church parade at the Cathedral - we sometimes went and it was a lovely service and you heard all those male voices. The Kent Cyclists' Battalion was stationed in South Canterbury and they used the crossroads at the junction of Nunnery Fields, Puckle Lane and South Canterbury Road as their parade ground. The Army were billeted in all the houses there - we had soldiers at No. 38 all through the war and I wonder now where mother put us all. Much of the Army Transport was horse-drawn, the barracks and horse lines were in the Military Road area and I can remember bolting horses running along the 'top of the town' as we called Broad Street and Upper Bridge Street. On Armistice Day we had all gone to school as usual in the morning and then the news came in later that the Armistice had been signed, so they shut the school immediately. Canterbury was one mass of people. There was a great service in the Cathedral in the afternoon and I think everyone went to that. Yes I can remember that day very well."

During Tom and Mary's childhood the firm was prosperous; there was work done maintaining windmills; the installation of alternative sources of power to that of wind; watermills were kept turning; teams went out to farms with ploughing tackle and with threshing machines; businesses large and small called on Holman Bros. for equipment and repairs; they were wheelwrights and built carts and wagons; the list is almost endless. Their father, Harry Branford and their uncle, William John, worked hard themselves; and one of their aunts, Fanny Holden helped her brothers in the office for a number of years - so it was a family business in the broadest sense not only for the Holmans themselves but among the employees - fathers and sons and brothers were to be found on the pay roll and it was a very stable work force.

In the nineteen thirties Harry Branford was helped more and more by his two sons, Frank and Tom, who had both served their five year apprenticeship in Lincolnshire. Mary trained as a teacher and taught at a boarding school for girls in Westmorland until 1947 when she returned to Canterbury to look after her parents and to continue teaching, this time at her old school, the Simon Langton Girls' School. Her elder sister, Doris, worked in Holmans office until her marriage in 1932 and because of this she did not go to University or make music her career although she was an accomplished pianist. Her marriage to Bert Hooker "united the well-known millwright's daughter with the well-known miller's son" - this miller was Alderman Frank Hooker the great Canterbury benefactor.

Many of Holmans employees started as apprentices and stayed with the firm all their working lives. Jim Knight told us it was "a good firm to work for; we all got on well together and those were happy times." It is from the memories of a few members of this work force that we have gained some insight into this firm which played such an important role in agriculture in East Kent in the early part of this century.

Harry Branford   William John

The two sons of Thomas Richard Holman

Map

- CITY WALL
- CATTLE MARKET
- UPPER BRIDGE STREET
- FLYING HORSE INN
- WILLIAM HOLMAN'S VEGETABLE GARDEN
- STEAM PLOUGHING AND THRESHING MACHINES PARKED
- HOL... MEAD...
- THE WHITE ELMS
- N ↑
- .12
- .13
- 14
- OLD DOVER ROAD
- VERNON GRAN...
- TOM HOLMAN'S ORCHARD AND BEEHIVES
- 100 YARDS
- MS 92
- 16
- 15
- .17
- 18

HOLMANS PREMISES BEFORE THE BLITZ

Key

Holmans property

* 1 Front Shop, 12 Dover Street
* 2 Office, 12 Dover Street
  ("OFFICE" still carved above the entrance)
* 3 Holmans Cottages, 13-16 Dover Street
  (let to employees)
4 Mounted plate for steel tyreing wooden wheels
5 Crane (erected after the war)
6 Sawmill
7 Works' Bell
8 Main Engineering Workshop
9 Chimney
10 Coalstore
11 Two-storey building: rope store above;
paint shop below (* some internal structures
preserved inside present postwar building)
* 12 Old lime tree
* 13 One surviving apple tree (a Bramley)
14 Double gates
15 Store for lifting gear and pulley wheels
16 Timbershed
17 Crane
* 18 General Store, including racks of foundry patterns (after 1942 this became the main
workshop until in 1954 a new large workshop was built in the centre of Holmans Meadow)

* indicates still standing 1992

Traction engine and threshing machine at the Dover Street workshops with Frank Edney

Walter Griffith describes to us how the ploughing was done - "There was a man called Wanston, he was one of the people who went out with a gang for ploughing. They would go off, two steam engines with a big plough; one engine was each side of the field and they'd pull the plough across with a great steel cable and then they'd turn the plough over so that one shear was in the ground and the other up in the air. They moved the engines along all the time and the edges of the field were rather flattened with their weight, like a sort of path." When it was time for the threshing Norman Harris says "It was quite a sight in the mornings to see the cavalcade going out from the Dover Street premises on their way to work at some farm. There was the engine towing the thresher, then the house van, a straw trusser and perhaps a water tank. It meant a lot of skilful driving but it wasn't fast and everyone else kept out of the way." Fred Waters takes up the story - "When the men came back to Dover Street at the end of a day the drivers matched their skills at driving their huge engines and all the towed equipment through the very narrow gateway into the meadow at the back of the workshops."

Only very occasionally did these enormous road locomotives come to grief. Norman Harris remembers old Jack Wood, a driver, who somehow slid his engine off the road into a ditch. William Holman came out to inspect and asked "What happened then Jack?" "Well I don't rightly know, sir - she must have gone and slithered on a horse turd!" Margaret Holman, Tom Holman's wife, tells of a runaway engine careering down Summer Hill in Harbledown, finally coming to rest after it had knocked over a tree and a lamppost. Holman Bros. had to replace the tree and were sent a bill for the lamppost!

Walter Griffith talking of the scenes at the farms when the teams went for the threshing describes circular ricks with the corn heads facing inwards to prevent them being eaten by the farm animals. The 'feeders' used pitchforks to throw the corn from the ricks into the big hopper which shook and sifted the grain, the drive coming from the steam engine through a system of belts and pulleys, the whole operation creating a great deal of noise and dust. There were four or five men in a gang and they slept in the house van while working several days at one farm. In his own words, "It was a bit rough and they didn't get extra for being away from home but they didn't worry about things like that in those days. Lucky to have a job. They had a good time with plenty of beer and the farmer fixed them up with food. They had a stove which had a little chimney coming out at the top. They were warm and quite happy."

Jim Knight remembers "Traction engines were always kept in a shining condition, but cleaning the brass INVICTA symbol was always a problem as it would get sooty from the nearby pipes behind the door on which the symbol was fixed. These big traction engines were still being used perhaps as late as the early 1950s but agricultural work was changing rapidly; for instance to do the steam ploughing of a field would involve at least four men, but with the coming of the tractor this could be done more quickly with just one man."

With the disappearance from Holmans of the steam engines and the threshing machines Mrs. Wood of the Dover Street Hardware Stores tells us - "so the mice which had overrun the nearby houses also disappeared - there were no longer the seeds of corn brought in on the wheels and parts of the thresher."

George Newport who worked for the firm from 1946 to 1958 tells us that during these years Holmans owned about ten steam engines, four ploughing machines and six threshing machines. They maintained and repaired all their own machines and machinery as well as being skilled in the maintenance and repair not only of windmills and watermills but balers, tractors and milking machines on the farms.

Threshing on local farms during the First World War

The demolition of Harbledown Mill in 1913

Another type of contract which Holman Bros. were called upon to undertake with their steam traction engines was heavy duty work such as demolition. In 1913 the well-known landmark just outside Canterbury, the Harbledown windmill, was deemed to be unsafe and Tom and Mary's father, Harry Branford, was given the job of demolishing it. This he did by means of pulling it over with steel hawsers from the winding drum of the engine. Tom as a small boy was concerned lest the mill should fall on to the adjacent strawberry field; Mary, who was at the local cinema, was surprised to see her own father on an early newsreel supervising the demolition of this lovely mill.

A present day reconstruction

Fred Waters was apprenticed to the firm in 1925 when he was fourteen, "I wanted to do my apprenticeship at Holman Bros. as a millwright because it involved metal work and woodwork. I served four weeks on trial, to show whether I was suitable, and then went with Mr. Harry Holman to a solicitor to sign indentures for five years apprenticeship and two years as an improver. There was a £30 premium to pay which was common practice in those days. I was just shown how to do things. I worked with Bob Barber and George Urry in the watermills at Wye near Ashford, at Barton Mill along the Sturry Road and Abbot's mill owned by Denne's in St. Radigund's.

One of the biggest mill fires in Canterbury was in 1933 when this mill was burnt down. I was going back to work from the breakfast half-hour which we had in my earlier days at Holmans when I saw a lot of smoke rising and someone shouted 'it's Denne's mill on fire'. I jumped on my bike to go and see it and it was a terrible fire. Several fire engines were pumping water on to it but much of the water blew away as steam owing to the heat. There were showers of sparks and burning wood as machinery from the upper floors crashed down to the lower floors. I could hear the plop, plop, plop of rats jumping into the river to make their escape. Water was sprayed on the Miller's Arms public house opposite which saved it from serious damage but the mill foreman's house which was attached to the mill in Mill Lane was badly damaged.

Abbot's Watermill (Denne's Mill)

Mr Harry Holman, Tom's father, was there watching the fire and appeared very distressed over it because he really loved these old mills in which much of his life had been spent in working and planning machinery repairs and installations. After clearing up all that remained of the mill was one of the water wheel shafts and two iron posts."

Fred Waters also gave us the following interesting account of the type of work millwrights tackled. "The Barton Mill was a flour mill and was owned by Kingsford & Co. One of the biggest jobs I can remember Holmans doing was to fit new massive cast iron gear wheels to both of the water wheel drive shafts. They were known as pit-wheels because owing to their large diameter part of the wheel was revolving in a pit made in the floor for that purpose. To mesh with the pit-wheels Bob Barber and I also had to fit smaller diameter wheels to the vertical shafts which drove the machinery up in the mill. A frequent job we had in the maintenance of both watermills and windmills was the fitting of new sets of wooden cogs in the gear wheels. In the older mills some of the gear wheels were made entirely of wood and others were cast iron but the outer rim of any wheel which was fitted with wooden cogs has rectangular mortices in it to hold these cogs. They were made from hard woods such as beech, apple or hornbeam and for a wheel operated in wet conditions, like the pit-wheel, oak was mostly used. The cogs were cut roughly to shape from planks in the workshops at Dover Street and then taken to the mill for fitting. The shank of the cog, which is the part that fits into the mortice, had to be hand-chiselled to a good fit and driven in tightly, otherwise it would soon work loose with the pressure of the drive."

The water wheel shaft and two iron posts

Millwrighting could be extremely hard work and George Urry was remembered by his son Richard "Coming home on winter evenings with his face blue with cold after working from 7 a.m. to dusk on one of the mills, perhaps at Herne, Chillenden, Barham or St. Margaret's Bay or at one of the many watermills on the river Stour."

Besides windmills, watermills, ploughing and threshing and before the days of piped water Holman Bros. also maintained many of the wells around Canterbury. Frank Morphett started work with the firm in 1915 when he was fifteen years old and knew many of these old wells. The first one he went down was at Cockering Farm; he described to us, as if it was but yesterday, how the men rigged up the winch at the top of the well and two of them lowered him down on the cradle to the pump where he took it apart. He tied the plungers and couplings on to the back of the seat and was pulled up again. There they repaired the parts, tied them on once more to the back of the seat and he was lowered to put the pump together again. He remembers that 1921 was the driest year when he went right to the bottom; he only reached the bottom during these very dry periods. He said "They generally used to ask me to go down when they had trouble - not being able to get water - a pump could pick up water thirty feet and no more but it will deliver it for a devil of a long way. Hence the reason for the pumps having to be down the well. Nothing is nice about well work. We used candles for well light. I knew one well up at Luton, Selling ... it was raining in on you all the time you were down there, surface springs."

Jim Knight and George Stedman remember going down the brick-lined well at Lower Hardres. This was about six feet in diameter and 365 feet deep, as deep as the Cathedral is high. The man would be let down the well on a cradle with a lighted candle; if the light went out the air was 'foul' and the man would be winched up again. Fresh air had then to be pumped down to replace the toxic gases. It would take about twenty minutes for the cradle with the man and his tools to reach the bottom. George Stedman says "There wasn't much room down there and it was very dark, looking up you could only see a small circle of light at the top of the well." Jim Knight says "We could sometimes do the repairs down there, perhaps fixing new cup leathers in the pump or making repairs to the pipes, but any serious faults involved lifting all the parts to the surface to be attended to in the Dover Street workshops." Jim Knight did a lot of work with Harry Friar "We worked by the light of a torch or a lead light and always we had to keep a candle alight so as to warn us of foul air." Alfie Ingleton on going down once injured his hands as the handle came off the winching gear at the top and to stop the cradle crashing down to the bottom, he had to hold on to the rods. Accidents, however, were very few. Jim Knight couldn't recall any accidents at work during the eighteen years he was at Holmans ... 'we were just careful'.

These men, Frank Morphett, Walter Griffith, Fred Waters, Bob Barber, Jim Knight, George Stedman and many others were skilled craftsmen in more than one field. Norman Harris told us "Holman Bros. could turn their hand to anything, no job was too small or too big for them to tackle."

Bert Hooker told us that "Holmans were also well-known as licensed valuers - there are numbers of records of valuations such as tenant's fittings in mills when a new miller took over from an outgoing tenant."

Tom Holman has written - "During the first fifty years of the firm's existence very few records remain of the activities undertaken but it is believed that they were mostly in connection with windmills and millwrighting, wheelwrights, building carts and wagons and allied activities. The first available record is a Sales Ledger covering the years from 1865 to about 1880."

A Few Entries from Early Sales Ledgers 1868 - 1876

		£.	s.	d.
1868 April 2	**Mr F Walker** Repairing perambulator		1	9
1871 Mar. 1	**Canterbury Incorporation** Repairing lawn roller	1	1	0
1872 Oct. 15	**Mr Bing, Chemist, St. George's Street** 1 extra strong soda water machine	45	0	0
1876 Jan. 17	**Mr Adsett, Gunsmith** Sawing out 260 gun stocks	2	3	4
1876 Sept. 18	**Mr Herbert Collard, Coal Merchant** 1 new strong coal cart on springs with side and front boards Writing name on front and varnishing	20	0 5	0 0
1877 July 7	**Right Hon. Lord Sondes** Ironwork for supporting tree at Cricket Ground. 2 swivel nuts with R & L hand threads, 4 screws chain & hooks, iron straps with long bolt, 14lbs. plate iron 4 iron wedges. Plumber fitting 26lbs. lead on tree.	8	3	4
1876 Aug. 24	**Mr Crohall, Ickham** A new hop press with dial weighing apparatus.	13	18	10

Driving Gears in Stelling Minnis Windmill

Bob Barber working on a 'midling' for Barham Mill

The ability of Holmans to 'turn their hand to anything' was due to the skill of the craftsmen they employed; millwrights, wheelwrights, pattern makers, blacksmiths, turners, carpenters and engineers. These men trained their apprentices so well that they in turn could go anywhere afterwards to get a job; the name Holmans was sufficient recommendation. But the firm will long continue to be remembered for its work in the building and maintenance of windmills. George Newport recalls the very large lengths of imported Scandinavian wood which were used for the shaft or spar of the sweeps. They were hoisted off the lorry by the crane and then shaped by Bob Barber using an adze. This excellent craftsman also made the gears and cogs which were such an integral part of the windmills and watermills. Frank Williams, a wheelwright, was in charge of the repair of carts and wagons. To make a wheel is an art in itself; the hub, felloes and spokes were made and once assembled were then put on the large mounted plate in the yard while the steel tyre was heated on an open wood fire by the blacksmiths - this was a two-man job as George Stedman well remembers. The steel rim had to be red hot before being put round the wooden wheel and pushed down tightly. "Then we threw buckets of water over it - it cracked like anything as the metal tightened and later we put a rivet through to fix it. It was a good job." George Wells, who was Bob Barber's apprentice, recalls how he learned to dress the grinding stones for the mills; when these round Peak stones came in they were chiselled with a tool called a millbill so that there was a slight slope down from the rim to the centre hole along which the ground flour would run. The millbill was held in a thrift, George Wells and Norman Harris told us, but Tom Holman says "interestingly enough all the firm's records call it a thriff."

Fred Waters talked to us of Holmans installing, maintaining and repairing machinery for breweries, sawmills, oasthouses, Williamson's Tannery, Abbott Bros. Dairy, St. Lawrence Laundry - the list appeared to be endless. Before the First World War most farms still had simple hand-turned machines in their barns for chaff cutting, wurzel and turnip slicing, oats and oil cake crushing and so on. During the 1920s the farmers called on Holmans to have these rather primitive machines converted to power drive by installing stationary petrol or paraffin engines. These drove a length of shafting and by belts and pulleys all the barn machinery could be set in motion as it was needed.

Sometimes a manufacturer was unable to supply a spare part for a machine for a customer who then came to Dover Street. Holmans would come to the rescue - a wooden pattern of the piece would be made and from this a casting was obtained which was finally finished in the engineering shop. One such customer was the owner of Dreamland in Margate and a number of parts for his amusement machines came from this source. Another was when the wheels and axles from the passenger lifts between Folkestone Leas and the lower road were brought in; these were mounted on the largest lathe (said to be the largest in East Kent) which trued up the wheels where grooves had been worn during the thousands of journeys the lifts had made.

An unusual invoice dated February 22nd 1863 was to Holman & Collard for £68 10s. 0d. for the repair of the tread mill at Canterbury Prison. This was used for pumping up the water and it was maintained by Holmans until its demolition. At this time the firm was a partnership of Holman & Collard for a brief period.

George Newport told us that the firm was sometimes called in for emergency work on the Cathedral organ. The brass bearings on the shaft which carried the blower and its blades could seize up, especially if the organ had been used on a Saturday or Sunday going full out. To get to these bearings to remove them for repair meant going up to the 'cat walk' which was very high up and very narrow. George remembers once having to carry out this work at 2 o'clock in the morning and the organist having to be there to play the organ to test the bearings.

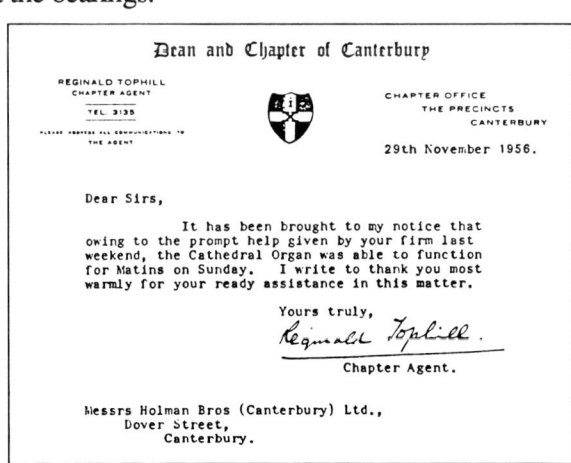

Mr. Harry Holman and his two sons, 'Mr. Frank' and 'Mr. Tom' as they were known, were responsible for the millwrighting, the workshops and the engineering side of the business. Mr. William Holman managed the agricultural side, the ploughing and the threshing. His son, Jack, was a windmill enthusiast from his schooldays and after leaving London University he worked with the family firm for about a year before being called up at the beginning of the 1939-45 war. He served in R.E.M.E. throughout the war, later becoming a full colonel and A.D.C. to H.M. the Queen for two years. He rejoined Holmans briefly but then left to pursue a career with British Petroleum.

In the nineteen twenties Holmans expanded and bought The White Elms in Old Dover Road with its one and a half acre meadow where they kept their huge traction engines and all the bulky agricultural equipment. They also bought a second piece of land (which they had rented for a number of years) in the Old Dover Road adjacent to what is now the Canterbury Health Centre.

By the beginning of the Second World War the main workshop was a two-storey timbered building, the lower floor housed the metal-working machines with work benches around the sides and a blacksmiths' section containing two forges. A spiral staircase led to the upper floor where there were three workshops with the well-remembered Holmans bell hanging outside. One part was the wheelwrights' shop where the wooden wheels for carts and wagons were made; another was the millwrights' shop and the remaining area was the carpenters' shop which was equipped with a circular saw, lathe, grinder and morticing machine.

Holmans Yard, Old Dover Road

Market days on Mondays and Saturdays when the farmers came into Canterbury were particularly busy. Holmans had a desk in the old Corn Exchange and "Harry Holman was a familiar figure every Saturday, meeting the farmers and taking their orders. Prices were agreed by word of mouth and nothing was written down." Tom Holman told us that "in the early thirties it was difficult getting your money from the farmers - there was no real recession in our line because agriculture was an essential business but the farmers had to rely on selling their corn once a year and until it was sold there wasn't much money available." Fred Waters told us "even if Holmans were short of work they never stood anyone off. We would service the contents of our tool chests by grinding edge tools and sharpening saws or by doing maintenance on machinery and equipment until work picked up again."

When asked if the office had a telephone Tom Holman said "I think we were one of the earliest who had a telephone in Canterbury - our old number was 108, then it changed to 2108 and then to 62108!"

Frank Morphett was an apprentice at Holman Bros. and stayed with the firm until his retirement. His daughter wrote "my grandfather had originally worked in Tenterden but when he heard that the wages in Canterbury were 1/6 a week more he and his wife set out on a journey that must have taken more than one day. They walked the whole way, he carrying all their belongings while his wife carried their baby son, Frank." Frank told us "I started at Holman Bros. in 1915 when I was fifteen years old. We lived at Patrixbourne and I would cycle to work leaving home at 5.30 a.m. to start work at 6 a.m. and finishing at 5 or 6 p.m. We had half an hour for breakfast and an hour for dinner. My wage then was 5/- a week. And then the war came along and they passed a Bill that apprentices should receive a living wage and mine went up to 27/6 a week. The Government said that it must be a living wage but the trouble was that it went on for a long time at 27/6 a week! There were about thirty men employed at Holmans in those days. When I started I did turning and screw cutting; you were with the older men watching and then they used to give you a job to do on your own. We took our own food usually but we could make tea on a little stove in one of the house vans."

Jim Knight when he started work at Holmans in 1941, also at the age of fifteen, was paid 14/- a week. He remembers working with Harry Friar down wells and Mrs. Friar told us that the men were paid half-a-crown an hour extra as danger money when they were doing this difficult work. The working hours then were from 7.30 a.m. to 5 p.m. with an hour off for dinner - this was an eight and a half hour working day compared with the nine and a half hours worked by Frank Morphett some twenty five years earlier. He remembers that in 1941 everyone at Holmans queued up outside the bottom office on Fridays for their pay and Mr. William Holman paid out. "The money was all ready in little piles of coins for each worker - pay packets came much later but when I left in 1961 I was earning £10 a week - good money for those days."

According to the records in 1891 the only holidays for the employees were the six Bank Holidays a year - the August holiday one was at that time known as the 'Bean Feast' - but in Jim Knight's time the men were entitled to two weeks paid annual holiday as well as the usual Bank holidays.

Holmans Annual Works Outing 1931

Throughout the years Holman Bros. always exhibited at the East Kent Agricultural Shows and later at the Kent Agricultural Shows when awards were invariably won by them. A week of excitement preceded these annual displays as agricultural equipment and new machinery were prepared for the three-day-event. Some of the men, such as Bert Benfield and his son, demonstrated the tractors and other machinery whilst the Holmans themselves were always there talking with the farmers, giving advice and taking orders.

For Holmans these were golden years: they were soon to be followed by the shattering events of the 1939-45 war.

Holmans Meadow before the Blitz

Holmans Meadow today

Air Raid Precautions in the Cathedral Nave 1939

Holman Bros. were directly concerned at the beginning of the Second World War in helping to strengthen the crypt of the Cathedral in order to provide an air raid shelter safe enough to withstand high explosives. The sides of the crypt were sandbagged. Thousands of tons of dry earth were also brought into the Cathedral and spread out over the crypt below. This earth was then covered with wooden planking which remained there until the end of the war. Norman Harris remembers helping to fix a small track up the sixteen steps leading from the nave to the quire and Tom Holman thinks that not many people can have had his experience of driving a car and trailer through the great west doors, taking a winch from his workshop to hoist up the trolleys of earth and the innumerable sandbags.

Norman Harris also recalls an occasion during the war when a 'dogfight' was taking place overhead while the Holman traction engines were steam ploughing near Swalecliffe. Bullets were flying everywhere and the man on the engine was so busy watching the aerial battle that the plough being hauled across the field crashed into one of the engines and had to have extensive repairs done back at the Dover Street workshop.

Between 1939 and 1945 over eight hundred buildings in Canterbury were destroyed and many thousands more were damaged. There was a fire-watching scheme at Holmans and a room at No. 13 Dover Street was turned into a fire-watchers' base where the two men whose turn it was to be on duty could make tea or even snatch some sleep if there was no air raid. However, in the early hours of 1st June 1942, Holmans workshops were directly hit by several dozen incendiaries and, being constructed of timber, they were soon completely destroyed. The flames spread to the nearby Nag's Head public house and as they took hold so they became blue in colour as the alcohol was released; but despite valiant efforts to save the building the Nag's Head was burned to the ground. The Holman cottages were threatened and the end gable was ablaze but the fire fighters, using their stirrup pumps and buckets of water, were just in time to bring the fire under control and to save the whole row from destruction.

Frank Clark was spending the last weekend of his embarkation leave with his parents who lived on the corner of Dover Street and Vernon Place where his father had a clock repairing business. He wrote this graphic description of that air raid: "Between 12.30 and 1.00 a.m. the danger siren was sounded and we took to the cellar. The raid started with the roar of dive bombers and a series of screeching whistles and crumps. Our ack-ack guns joined in. The house shook so much that we could not rest our heads against the wall. Our only light was the eerie glow that came through the cellar grating. There were lulls but then new waves of bombers took over. It sounded as if there was a lot of activity all around, and then no more bombs after that. We looked out. We were surrounded by flames, luckily for us at a reasonable distance and mainly downwind. In Dover Street Holmans engineering yard and the Nag's Head were blazing - tiles were crashing off roofs and a petrol pump went up in a big explosion. Streets were strewn with tiles, glass and ashes." Frances Aitken came out of the underground shelter in her garden at Vernon Grange and described what she found. "The air was thick, thick, thick with oily smoke caused by the nearby fires at Holmans workshops and their burning stores of oil. This black smoke got everywhere - our hair was thick with it - and there was no water at all to wash in!"

Reproduced by permission of the Kent Messenger Group

The lower end of Dover Street after the Air Raid of 1st June 1942

After this air raid most of Holmans employees turned up for work as usual - work which involved clearing up and trying to rescue what they could from the smouldering ruins. Some of the machinery was totally destroyed but what could be salvaged was taken across to their Old Dover Road premises and work carried on from there. The power hammer, a couple of lathes, the power saws and a drilling machine were able to be saved. Jim Knight tells us that a temporary workshop in Dover Street was soon built around what remained of the original forge and chimney and a few years after the war a large single-storey workshop was erected in the middle of Holmans Meadow.

Since 1854 a large brass bell had hung outside the carpentry section of the workshops and it was a well-remembered sound in pre-war Canterbury as it rang out at the start and close of each working day. It was feared that the bell had been completely destroyed in the fire but miraculously it was later found - half of it had melted away in the intense heat of the burning buildings during the devastating raid, but the clapper and the remaining half, still proudly bearing the date 1854 is now one of Tom Holman's prized possessions.

Holmans Bell

Like so many other businesses in Britain after the war, Holmans had to rebuild and adapt to many changes: changes in the type of work undertaken, to new technology and to new working practices. As Jim Knight put it, "because combine harvesters were coming on to the farms the old threshing machines and with them the 'gangs' that went out with them were no longer needed." George Newport recalled that in 1949 Holmans received their first combine harvester from America. It was delivered in crates and created a great stir when it was unpacked and assembled at the Dover Street premises. And, in 1951 the first pick-up automatic baler arrived - also from America. Other firms coming into the area brought more competition but the Holman workshops continued to be busy with repair work to tractors and combines. The firm became local agents for International Harvesters, Fergusons and Massey Harris. On a smaller scale they repaired and maintained motor mowers used on golf courses, on bowling greens and in gardens and on the agricultural side the gang mowers, which were pulled by tractors and were used in orchards.

Harry Branford died in 1950 at the age of nearly eighty-seven and Jim Knight remembers "old Mr. Harry Holman was a very familiar figure as he kept coming down to the works right to the end of his life." Then in 1954 William John died at the age of ninety. The local press described him as "Canterbury's oldest business man" and reported that he had attended his business regularly until three weeks before his death. Perhaps 'Mr. Frank' and 'Mr. Tom' on reading these reports thought back to their great-grandfather John Holman starting the firm in 1816, of it being carried on by his sons, John James and Thomas Richard. Then to Thomas Richard's two sons, these two grand old Canterbury business men who had carried on right up to their recent deaths. Would they have thought now about the future of Holman Bros.? It had always been a family business; its prosperity stemming from the earlier generations' love and work with windmills and millwrighting yet having the foresight to adapt to changes in meeting the needs of the farming community so that the sons could carry on as their fathers handed over to them. But now the chain would be ended - the next generation had chosen other careers.

Frank Holman wished to retire in about 1966 so all the Dover Street buildings and Holmans Meadow were sold to Sloggetts the builders. But Tom Holman kept the Old Dover Road premises and the firm's work continued from there. His employees have many memories of him during these postwar years; Norman Harris says "he was a whizz-kid with electrical work - he would say to his men 'now this will either work or it won't' - and it usually did!" George Newport describes him as a brilliant mathematician and mechanic and all told us 'those were happy times.' But in 1975 Tom Holman decided to retire and, sadly it seems to us, the family firm which was so much a part of the Canterbury scene for over one hundred and fifty years was put up for sale.

At the time of the sale we were told that "Holmans could have long continued as there was always a need for repairs to tractors and combines and so on." Malcolm Hobbs said "for the sale everything was perfect, all the equipment was polished and the tools sharpened; Holman Bros. were always perfectionists and the whole works should have been kept as a living museum."

Throughout this story we have seen that the members of the family had always recognised the changes which took place over the whole range of agriculture, especially as it affected them in East Kent and in Canterbury in particular. In 1955 the cattle market moved from where it had been near Dover Street since at least 1580 and several small industries and workshops also moved away. Dover Street itself was steadily becoming a more residential area with a sprinkling of offices and quiet shops, such a contrast to the busy hive of activity that it was in Holmans heyday. With this changing environment and without the next generation to continue the family business it is not surprising that Tom Holman decided that the final chapter in the long history of Holman Bros. had been reached.

But their name will continue in Dover Street. In 1992 the car park which now occupies the site once owned by Holman Bros. has been renamed HOLMANS MEADOW by the City Council and a plaque is to be placed there to commemorate the firm which became part of Canterbury's heritage.

The Society acknowledges with gratitude the following people who have helped with this publication:

Bernard Barber, Raymond Beaulieu, Frank Clark, Liz Clement, Ken Cole, Robin Colyer, Pam Dagwell, Elizabeth Friar, Harold Gough, Walter Griffith, Jean Harbour, Norman Harris, Malcolm Hobbs, Robert Hobbs, P.S. Jarvis, Tony Jarvis, Timothy Keenan, Jim Knight, Clare McLaren, George Newport, George Stedman, Brian Stewart, Jim Styles, Fred Waters, George Wells, Dennis Whiting, Beryl Wood, Richard Urry.

Tom Holman

REFERENCES

William Coles Finch. 'Watermills and Windmills: A Historical Survey of their Rise, Decline and Fall as Portrayed by those of Kent' (1933: reprinted 1976)

B.J. and J.M. Turpin. 'Windmills in Kent' (1979)

Jenny West. 'The Windmills of Kent' (1973)